King Cromwell

A play

Oliver Ford Davies

Samuel French — London
New York - Toronto - Hollywood

CHARACTERS

Oliver Cromwell: Lord Protector of England, Scotland and Ireland; 58
John Thurloe: Secretary of State; 41
Frances Lambert: John Lambert's wife; 35
Bettie Claypole: Oliver's daughter; 28
Richard Cromwell: Oliver's eldest surviving son; 31
John Lambert: Second-in- command of the Army; 38
Andrew Marvell: tutor and poet; 38
Edward Sexby: former colonel and leveller; 42

The musician, John Hingston, is never seen

The action takes place in the Palace of Whitehall, London, at the end of Cromwell's life in 1657

KING CROMWELL

First presented at the Orange Tree Theatre, Richmond, on 12th November 2003, with the following cast:

Oliver Cromwell	Oliver Ford Davies
John Thurloe	Hugh Simon
Frances Lambert	Miranda Foster
Bettie Claypole	Claudia Elmhirst
Richard Cromwell	Damien Matthews
John Lambert	Paul Goodwin
Andrew Marvell	Sean Baker
Edward Sexby	John Ashton

Directed by Sam Walters
Designed by Sam Dowson
Lighting by Kevin Leach
Stage managed by Stuart Burgess, Sophie Acreman, Samantha Tagg and Hannah Wye

AUTHOR'S NOTE

The play is fiction. It certainly couldn't all have happened on one single day. Some of these scenes undoubtedly took place, but we have virtually no record of what was said in them. At the same time all the facts referred to in the play are true — whether the offer of the crown, the succession issue, Lambert's ambition, Richard's painting, Bettie's feud with Frances, Marvell's secretaryship, Sexby's pamphlet and capture, Thurloe's spies, Hingston's music, or Davenant's operas. A significant amount of what Cromwell, Marvell and Sexby say in the play is taken from their writings and speeches, but a great deal is invented. I doubt if the real characters had such a clear analysis of what was going on in 1657, but then that is the inevitable prerogative of history plays — to add a degree of hindsight to the proceedings.

Between 1649 and 1660 England had a major revolution, followed by a republic. It is a period that has always fascinated me, particularly because the English revolutionaries, unlike their American, French and Russian successors, had no Rousseau or Marx to guide them. They made it up as they went along. A great debate took place, thousands of pamphlets were written, daring experiments in government were attempted. Cromwell seems to me to exemplify the search, the experiment, and the ultimate failure. He was a mass of contradictions. He was a military dictator searching for a democratic basis for his rule. He was a religious fundamentalist seeking godly reformation, who also believed in a broad tolerant national church. He was a resolute parliamentarian who held free elections and then excluded the opposition. He was a leader of unassailable authority who could find no-one comparable to succeed him. All these are major 20th, and probably 21st century themes. In all the confusions of his conservative radicalism/radical conservativism, Cromwell is a very English political figure.

Oliver Ford Davies

ACT I

The Palace of Whitehall, London. 1657

The scene is a room, or a space with or without walls. There are a door; a table and chairs; and a bed

Thunder, which continues intermittently throughout the act

Cromwell, in a grey nightshirt, is asleep on the bed, the covers in disarray — it's been a bad night. There is a particularly loud clap of thunder. He starts, sits up, peers about him uncertainly. He slowly gets out of bed and stands, a tall, bulky figure, high colour in his face and nose, long straggly brown hair flecked with grey

He crosses and tries the door, but it's locked. He thumps on it. Muttering under his breath he looks around the room. He kneels by the bed and starts to pray

After a moment, a key turns in the lock. He tenses, as if to defend himself

Thurloe enters, sober bureaucrat and spymaster, always awash with papers

Cromwell Thurloe!
Thurloe Your Highness.
Cromwell Don't let the Scots in.
Thurloe Certainly not, Your Highness.
Cromwell I won't speak to the Kirk.
Thurloe No.

Beat

Cromwell This is not my room. Is it?
Thurloe No.
Cromwell Why am I here?
Thurloe Your bed. There was an explosion.
Cromwell Explosion?
Thurloe Gunpowder had been placed under your bed. It went off early…
 praise be!

Cromwell Where was I?

Thurloe Addressing the parliament. General Lambert thought it best kept a secret.

Cromwell From me?

Thurloe You in particular. You're to keep on the move.

Cromwell But ... why so far?

Thurloe Far?

Cromwell Why Edinburgh? I hate Scotland.

Beat

Thurloe You're in your palace, Your Highness.

Cromwell In ... Whitehall?

Thurloe Yes.

Cromwell Not in Scotland?

Thurloe No.

Cromwell No Kirk?

Thurloe The war is over, Your Highness. Six years.

Beat

Cromwell Whose room is this?

Thurloe Your son Richard sometimes sleeps here when he's in London.

Cromwell Might have known — feather mattress. Didn't get a wink. Who put me here?

Thurloe General Lambert. It's for your safety. Too many attempts on your life. He's doubled the guard on every door. You are not to leave the palace and not to visit Hampton Court.

Cromwell I can ride in the park?

Thurloe No.

Cromwell I'm a prisoner.

Beat

Thurloe The Parliament want their answer.

Cromwell They're not still here?

Thurloe The storm was so fierce they slept in the gallery. The Strand's under water, and there's no way through to Chelsea.

Cromwell Give them a boat.

Thurloe The current's too strong.

Cromwell I need time.

Thurloe It's their fifth time of asking. And I think their last. If you want to be king, you must decide today.

Beat

Cromwell Any news of Blake?
Thurloe None. The Spanish fleet may have given him the slip. He could be in Jamaica still.
Cromwell He could be dead. I'm going back to my room.
Thurloe You can't. Lambert's ripped out the floorboards.
Cromwell Why?
Thurloe Searching for gunpowder.

Cromwell groans

We cannot risk your life, Your Highness.
Cromwell Ay, none of you are quite ready for me to die yet.
Thurloe (*producing two pamphlets*) "Killing No Murder".
Cromwell What?
Thurloe (*reading*) "To Your Highness justly belongs the honour of dying for the people... and it cannot choose but be an unspeakable consolation to you in the last moments of your life to consider with how much benefit to the world you are like to leave it."
Cromwell Who wrote that?
Thurloe Edward Sexby. He's on the loose again, handing these out.
Cromwell Never remember Sexby having a sense of humour.
Thurloe Gunpowder under your bed?
Cromwell Hm. Good soldier. Enlisted with me at Huntingdon, second year of the war. Never stopped talking about revolution ... overturning ... king, church, law — everything. And I was the man to do it.
Thurloe And now killing you is no murder. We know he's in the pay of Spain. He'd rather the Stuarts were back on the throne.
Cromwell Why, Thurloe? Why?
Thurloe He claims you're "the greatest tyrant in history, surpassing Nebuchadnezzar."
Cromwell Leveller claptrap.
Thurloe All his Levelling breed have turned assassin. Or Quaker. I don't know which is worse.
Cromwell God still has work for me to do in this world. It's no part of his plan that I should be murdered by Edward Sexby.
Thurloe Amen.
Cromwell Where's my music?
Thurloe Mr Hingston's at choir practice.
Cromwell Fetch him. Tell him to bring his instrument. And I need breakfast.
Thurloe Papers to sign.

Thurloe puts papers to be signed on the table, bows and exits

Cromwell pushes them aside, and takes up the pamphlet

Cromwell "At your death you will be shown the greatest tyrant in history, surpassing Nebuchadnezzar." Sexby, how can you write such turd? (*He finds his clothes by the bed and starts to pull his nightshirt over his head*)

Frances Lambert, an attractive voluptuous woman, enters

Cromwell hurriedly pulls his nightshirt down, and stares at her. She takes off a wet cloak; underneath she has an elegant low cut dress

Frances Good. I've found you. I almost had to swim here.
Cromwell Lady Lambert.
Frances I know, I know. I shouldn't have come. But Thurloe will cover for us.
Cromwell Does he know...?
Frances Of course. How else would I have found you?
Cromwell And your husband?
Frances He didn't send me, Noll.

Cromwell sits heavily

What's the matter?
Cromwell Just a little giddy.
Frances (*feeling his forehead*) You've a fever.
Cromwell It comes and goes.
Frances Have the doctors seen you?
Cromwell There's nothing they can do. Sit by me, Frances. I can't give you much time.
Frances I came to see you about John.
Cromwell He's put me in this terrible room.
Frances He's obsessed about your safety.
Cromwell I preferred it when it was gardening.

They laugh

Frances Do you know he has a new tulip — a golden one? He wants to show it to the Dutch.
Cromwell It'd start a new war. What's the next colour?
Frances Black.
Cromwell Black!
Frances I know. Who would want a black flower? But black is to be the crown.

Cromwell I teased him once about his tulips. He's never spoken of them to me again.

Frances Hates being teased. A true Yorkshireman.

Cromwell (*laughing*) He was never happy in the Fens, was he?

Frances No. Too much sky. The land's so flat, you're forced to look at the heavens.

Cromwell No bad thing.

Frances It makes you a little crazy.

Cromwell Perhaps.

Frances John looks at the ground.

Cromwell Where battles are won.

Frances But not where imagination is found. John has none.

Cromwell No.

Frances John is no Cromwell. But there is no-one else to succeed you.

Beat

Cromwell Frances, I've not long to live …

Frances Noll! Doctors are wrong …

Cromwell All the time. But I feel it myself now. This palace has become my tomb.

Frances Then leave today. Come and stay with us at Wimbledon. We miss you. The children wonder where you are. They still treasure the games you gave them.

But Cromwell won't be drawn

You used to confide in me — remember? Four years ago. Whether you should become Protector.

Cromwell Ay.

Frances John was away in Yorkshire.

Cromwell I haven't forgotten.

Frances You said many things.

Cromwell Best not to remember.

Frances You said it was your dearest wish that I should one day be first lady in the land. And you had it in your power to make John your successor.

He is silent

But now you are to be king?

Cromwell Nothing is decided.

Frances The gallery is stuffed with Parliament men — no, they didn't see me — all waiting your answer.

Cromwell Let them wait.
Frances If you take the crown, your family succeeds you. That means King
   Richard.

He is silent

You're angry with me.
Cromwell No, I think of nothing else.
Frances Then follow your nose.
Cromwell (*touching his large nose*) Not difficult. You once said it was a
   beacon to all England.

They both laugh. Cromwell touches her

My jewel.
Frances Noll, stay Protector ... and nominate John when the time comes ...

*Bettie rushes in — spirited, attractive, six months pregnant, in a rich
dressing-gown. Richard follows in an elegant but battered suit. He has a
sensitive, delicate face*

Bettie At last! (*She embraces Cromwell*)
Cromwell Bettie. Richard.
Richard Father.
Bettie I've opened every chamber door in Whitehall. Some surprises, I can
   tell you ... (*She sees Frances*) Oh! Lady Lambert.
Frances (*slightest of curtsies*) Lady Elizabeth, Lord Richard.
Bettie What an early call.
Frances My husband was concerned about His Highness' quarters.
Bettie He chose this awful room?
Richard I sleep here sometimes.
Bettie Exactly. And why did General Lambert not have the courtesy to
   consult any of His Highness' family?
Frances The fewer people who knew the better. The assassins may still be
   in the palace.
Bettie I see. Just Lambert, Thurloe ... oh, and Lady Lambert. And where
   does my father drag his mattress tonight?
Frances Your father's safety is paramount ...
Bettie (*losing her temper*) Are you to be the judge of that? You hold no
   position at court, Lady Lambert. Nor are like to do so.
Frances His Highness needs support ...
Bettie His Highness' needs will be supplied by his family.
Frances (*becoming reckless*) Naturally, but I have known Oliver since you
   were a child ...

Cromwell I think Lady Lambert has other pressing duties.

Beat

Frances If Your Highness says so. I found it wise to rest until noon when I was in your condition, my dear.
Bettie Your Ladyship has had ample practice.
Frances (*with a low curtsy*) Your Highness.

Frances exits with as much dignity as possible

Bettie lets out a cry of exasperation

Cromwell I'm told you and she screamed at one another last week. Like Billingsgate fishwives.
Bettie She maddens me beyond my patience. She sweeps about the court as if Lambert was already his highness.
Cromwell Well, no more of Frances Lambert.
Bettie Oh Father, she has charmed you out of your reason. And will charm her husband into the succession.
Richard Bettie …
Bettie I know.
Cromwell I need my breakfast.
Bettie Mother has left strict orders — fish, eggs, leeks …
Cromwell Leeks — I'm not that ill.
Bettie And asses' milk.
Cromwell Asses' milk!
Bettie Mother has ordered a dozen asses to be kept in Green Park.
Cromwell Your mother is at Hampton and will never know. (*To Bettie*) Unless somebody tells her. Now, leave me. I have work to do.
Richard Father, we came to see you on Fanny's behalf. She was in tears last night about her marriage.
Cromwell There is to be no marriage.
Richard Why not?
Cromwell Robert Rich is not a welcome suitor. He's given to gaming and … such-like things.
Bettie Nonsense.
Richard Father, they love one another.
Bettie So Robert Rich is no longer good enough, useful enough. Fanny is to be bait for the biggest catch of all.
Cromwell What catch?
Bettie The prince over the water. Who is not of course given to gaming and such-like things.

Cromwell What's this?

Bettie The court talks of nothing else. Charles Stuart is to be Cromwell's new
son-in-law ... and restored to the throne on Cromwell's conditions. A very
English settlement.

Cromwell Charles Stuart is so damnably debauched he would undo us all.
Give him a whore and a shoulder of mutton, that's all he cares for. He's like
his father — promise anything and break his word at the first chance. If he
ever returned, we should all end up on the gallows — from prison or the
grave. No more of him. Bettie, you should be in bed.

Bettie But I'm bored. The children are at Hampton, my husband's running
errands for you in Norfolk ...

Richard Bettie, you must rest.

Bettie I can't stay in bed for three months.

Cromwell The doctors tell me you may not survive another stillbirth.

Bettie Oh. What do they know? (*She kisses Cromwell*) Come and talk to me.

Cromwell Ay, later.

Bettie And dress yourself. You look like a mad hermit.

Bettie exits

Richard is about to follow

Cromwell Dick, stay.

*Richard stays. Cromwell begins a series of exercises, swinging his legs and
arms*

Richard Is this wise, in your state, Father?

Cromwell I'm cooped up here, a prisoner. I need exercise.

Richard A run in the long gallery?

Cromwell With twenty Parliament men relishing my every groan? Queen
Bess did half an hour's galliard before breakfast every day.

Richard Well, a little dancing, perhaps ...

Cromwell I tell you the galliard's a deal more tiring than this. I tried it once
— it nearly killed me.

Richard Even so ...

Cromwell I suppose you need money?

Richard A hundred pounds would help.

Cromwell sighs

Fifty?

Cromwell Ten years you've been in debt. Horses, paints, canvasses ...

Richard Men take advantage of me because I'm your son.

Cromwell If you weren't my son, you'd be rotting now in a debtor's prison.

Richard If I weren't your son, I'd stay in the country ...

Cromwell And paint pictures.

Richard And paint pictures. It's a country pleasure. You hawked, I paint.

Cromwell finishes his exercises

Cromwell Ay, but I worked too. I had to. I knew when to sow, what every acre should bear, how many lambs to send to market. I had no father to give me a hundred pounds...

Richard So you've often told me.

Beat

Cromwell I need you to do more in the world.

Richard I'm a member of Parliament.

Cromwell You rarely attend.

Richard Have you heard the standard of debate?

Cromwell I made you a Commissioner.

Richard Ay, for Trade and Navigation. They're exciting mornings I can tell you. I sit there and tell the burghers of Watchet their harbour has silted up.

Cromwell It's called government. (*Placatingly*) Dick, I wish you to be better known. I'm still ... Chancellor of Oxford — you could have that.

Richard Would I have to give them a lecture?

Cromwell No, just a feast. That's the only thing they understand. Twenty dozen bottles of port, and they'll call you the greatest intellect in Europe. And it's time you had a regiment.

Richard I couldn't get 'em to march, let alone fire at the enemy.

Cromwell Lambert could teach you in a week.

Richard I don't think the great Lord Johnny takes kindly to my sudden advancement.

Cromwell Lambert will do what he's told.

Richard Indeed.

Cromwell Now your brother Henry accepted a regiment as soon as ——

Richard Oh ay — Henry. I never stop hearing how well Henry does. A true son of Cromwell, couldn't wait to join the army. Now he's in Ireland, busy seizing their land and transporting them to God knows where ...

Cromwell Rebels have to be punished, soldiers have to be paid. Dick, listen to me. If I accept the crown, you would be my heir.

Richard Henry would make a better fist of it.

Cromwell A monarchy that starts choosing among its children is a monarchy half lost already.

Richard Then so be it.

Cromwell Your heart is hardly in it.

Richard Your heart is hardly in naming me. What has happened to your beloved Johnny? If only he were my elder brother. Perhaps you could pass a decree? Or Thurloe could discover some statute of Alfred's ...

Cromwell Everything is a jest to you, isn't it?

Richard Father, what would I do as king? The army won't back me — Lambert especially. Parliament patronizes me ... The godly despise me. There'd be a civil war within a year.

Cromwell The army'd be loyal to you — I'll see to that.

Richard I'm sure ... Purge 'em till they squeak. I warn you now, Father, I'll have no blood spilled on my account. I won't destroy the life of the least person in this land to preserve my greatness. Greatness which is a burden to me already.

Cromwell Which is a burden to all of us.

Richard Ay, but at least you earned yours. From backbencher and lowly captain. Mine is thrust upon me, when all men can see I have done nothing to deserve it. Surely not the intention of Providence?

Cromwell God may use improbable means.

Richard Ay, improbable.

Cromwell Dick, knowledge of Providence is the highest happiness. Faith gives us a sure certainty.

Richard Father, you know that you are in a state of grace, that you are of the Elect. But I have no such sure certainty.

Cromwell You have faith.

Richard (*hesitantly*) Yes.

Cromwell With faith, there is nothing to be feared but our own sin and sloth. God brought us here not to sit at home, but to consider what work we may do in the world. You are the son that God has spared me, and you will take up my inheritance.

Richard Father, don't persist. I'll never be a second Cromwell, the strong man of Europe, the greatest general England has ever known. Do you know there's a pamphlet circulating doubting I am your son?

Cromwell What!

Richard Thurloe kept that from you, did he?

Cromwell Never dare speak of your mother ...

Richard Oh, Mother's virtue is the stuff of legend. No, I am some aberration, some cuckoo. How could Cromwell's son be a born idler? Father, whatever you decide about the crown, don't waste it on me. Make Lord Johnny your successor. He and his lady dream of nothing else. He'll seize it when the time comes, whatever we intend. I'm sure that's all part of the divine plan — don't you think?

Richard exits

A beat

Cromwell (*calling*) Hingston, are you there yet?

A trill on the harpsichord outside the door

Oh, thank God! Play me something familiar.

Hingston starts to play "Gather ye Rosebuds". Cromwell starts to dress, in a plain grey suit

"Gather ye rosebuds". That's a dismal song. Robert Herrick. I was at Cambridge with him. Always writing filthy verses to his mistress instead of reading the scriptures. Still does, I expect. Hingston, who wrote the tune — William Lawes?

An affirmative trill

I thought so. Good musician. Royalist, mind. Killed in '45 ... at Bristol ... no, Chester. Waste. (*Calling*) Play something with spirit. And none of your New Music. I pay you a hundred a year, and all I get is Monteverdi, Schutz ... Scheidt (*pronounced "Shite"*). I won't have 'em, do you hear? No Scheidt before breakfast.

Hingston starts to play "All in a Garden Green", a version of the Diggers' anthem

That's better. (*Singing along*) "Stand up now, and the poor shall wear the crown, so stand up now ..." Leveller cant ... Sexby used to plague me with it. One man, one vote. Free meat and drink and clothes. Knock down the cathedrals and give the money to the poor. They thought they could achieve Utopia. (*Singing*) "Stand up now, stand up now." (*Speaking*) Ay for anarchy and chaos. But at least it has a tune. And it's English. And it's not Scheidt. That's enough! I must work. A march!

Cromwell sits at the table, and looks at the papers. Hingston starts to bang out the "Scots March"

John Lambert enters; good-looking, long hair, richly dressed, much like the traditional Cavalier. He listens for a moment

Lambert The "Scots March". We played it at Dunbar. I can see you now, biting your lip, blood running down your chin, laughing out loud and crying, "The Lord of Hosts is with us ..."

Cromwell "The God of Jacob is our refuge."
Lambert "Let God arise and let his enemies be scattered."
Cromwell "Let them also that hate him flee before him."
Lambert "As smoke is driven away, so drive them away."
Cromwell "As wax melteth before the fire, so let the wicked perish at the presence of God."
Lambert } (*together*) "Sing unto God, sing praises to his name."
Cromwell }
Lambert It was a mad chance. We were outnumbered, cut off, backs to the sea. And you *attacked*. Unbelievable.

They both laugh

Cromwell In an hour they were routed, hundreds dead, ten thousand prisoner.
Lambert I don't believe we lost twenty men. The army loved you that day.
Cromwell Because they saw I had Providence on my side.
Lambert Some of them called it luck. Always follow a lucky general.
Cromwell Found barrels of it, did you?
Lambert Barrels?
Cromwell Gunpowder. Under my floorboards.
Lambert Not as yet, Noll.
Cromwell Arrested anyone?
Lambert I'm questioning the entire household.
Cromwell That's why there's no breakfast.
Lambert No-one could have entered your chamber without a servant's help.
Cromwell It was probably Sexby. Seen this? (*He hands Lambert the pamphlet*) He walked straight past your guards dragging a barrel of gunpowder, and they saluted.
Lambert We've had reports of Edward Sexby.
Cromwell Where?
Lambert Bristol, Canterbury … Norwich.
Cromwell Ah well, that narrows it down.
Lambert We shall catch him.
Cromwell Probably at the palace gates, handing out these.
Lambert The gallery's full of people. Could have been any of them.
Cromwell Parliamentary delegation. Been there three days.
Lambert Terrible smell.
Cromwell One privy between 'em.
Lambert Lobbying by stench.

They laugh

Cromwell How's your brood at Wimbledon?
Lambert Colic, coughs, the mumps. Two or three are always ill.
Cromwell How many is it now?
Lambert Nine. Or ten.

They both laugh

Cromwell And the Lord has spared them all. You and Frances are blessed.
Lambert She sends her love.
Cromwell She was here earlier.
Lambert Frances?
Cromwell She asked me to refuse the crown. And nominate you Protector.
Lambert She had no right to interfere.
Cromwell She's loyal to her husband.

Lambert is very uncomfortable, but he plunges in

Lambert Three years ago you told me I was your heir.
Cromwell Ay.
Lambert I was as good as proclaimed your successor.
Cromwell And you may be yet.
Lambert What do you want with new titles? You hate them. You're already His Highness Lord Protector. You're king in all but name.
Cromwell It's the name Parliament lust after.
Lambert Let 'em lust. The people have no lust for monarchy.
Cromwell The people have no lust for this republic.
Lambert Maybe not — but with certain changes …
Cromwell Oh, changes! The people are sick of your everlasting changes, John — your major generals — your constitutions …
Lambert It was my constitution that made you protector. And without further change the republic will not survive your …
Cromwell Death? I know. I see you all, circling overhead.
Lambert Charles Stuart is circling Ireland with a fleet.
Cromwell John, the people understand tradition. King and Parliament. They want settlement in a tradition known to them.
Lambert Tradition! What tradition were we upholding when we cut off the king's head? When we rid ourselves of lords and bishops? The army did that, and small thanks to Parliament.
Cromwell There must be a Parliament.
Lambert The army made this republic, plain men who had the courage to fight for what they believed. And the republic will last just as long as the army supports it. Parliament won't save it — not by a single day. They've neither the will nor the strength. They'd sooner ask Charles Stuart back.

Cromwell Parliament is fundamental.

Lambert The fundament, more like. Very well, if it's tradition you long for, then recall the rump of your precious Long Parliament, and let them rule the country again.

Cromwell The Rump! The Rump! They were jugglers, drunkards — whoremasters, set on one thing — procuring jobs and flesh for their relations. Four years we let 'em rule the republic, and what did they achieve? Fatter fees for lawyers! I tell you that farting Rump had but one intent — to stay in power for all eternity. I knew the Lord had finished with 'em — so I went down to their House ... I took away their mace, their bauble, and my soldiers cleared 'em out ... I had no thought to do it when I arrived — but feeling the hand of God so strong upon me ... I kicked their backsides going ... (*He tries to demonstrate kicking, reels, and falls speechless*)

Lambert Noll! Noll!

Thurloe enters immediately

He's taken ill.

Thurloe (*examining him*) He is often thus. When provoked.

Lambert I'd no thought to ...

Thurloe Help me get him on to the bed. Take his feet. Gently. Gently. He was confused when I found him this morning. Didn't want to meet the Kirk — thought he was in Scotland.

Lambert Scotland!

Thurloe There are two thousand rooms in Whitehall. If you make him sleep in a different one each night, God knows where he'll think he is. Scotland, Ireland — Jamaica.

Lambert I think we should send for Dr Bate ...

Cromwell sits up on the bed

Cromwell No. No doctors. If I'd listened to doctors I'd have been in my grave years since. It's this damned stone — when I try to piss, it cuts me in two ... It feels like a tennis ball ...

Lambert You should see a surgeon.

Thurloe It's too soon to risk the knife again. You must rest, Your Highness.

Cromwell (*striding about, though staggering*) It's not rest I need — it's violence ... I need to ride in my coach and hit every rut and pothole from here to Hampton — anything to shift it an inch or two ... I am no man's prisoner ... I'm going to find my room.

Cromwell lurches out of the door

Thurloe Your Highness, there's no floor …
Lambert He'll find out soon enough.

A beat, while Thurloe gathers up papers

   Does he mean to be king?
Thurloe He twists this way and that.
Lambert Naturally.
Thurloe One moment Tamburlaine the Great, the next …
Lambert The Archangel Gabriel?

They laugh

Thurloe Last week he was the Village Constable.
Lambert Humility — I don't like that. He's much happier blaming everyone
   but himself.
Thurloe I've stopped guessing which role he'll give us next.
Lambert I gave up long ago. Just wait for the wind to change.
Thurloe It changes too often these days. His melancholy gets worse. And
   he has to give Parliament their answer. Today.
Lambert Today? Well, he's a master at putting off decisions.
Thurloe Except when the mania takes him. It's only then we get things done.
Lambert But the mania doesn't sustain him like it used to. It weakens him
   in minutes. How ill is he?
Thurloe He has a year or two at most. Providence will decide.
Lambert Providence has always decided mightily conveniently for Oliver.
   When he invokes Providence it's a sure sign he's going to change his mind.
Thurloe True.
Lambert Though I notice we hear less about the second coming of Christ
   these days.
Thurloe Don't underestimate Oliver's trust in godly reformation. He still
   believes England can be saved for Christ.
Lambert Oliver's lost his way. He was only really happy leading an army.
   He'd be at peace now if he'd let the army take charge.
Thurloe England will never submit to military rule.
Lambert England will submit to any rule Oliver chooses.
Thurloe Perhaps. But we have to find a rule that will survive him.
Lambert Ay. My fear is, he'll never make up his mind — and bring the
   whole thing down. He'll die, and nothing will be in place.
Thurloe Then we must ensure that it is. We must keep together. It's not
   Charles and his drunken exiles that will bring us down. It's divisions
   among ourselves.
Lambert Amen to that.

Thurloe Oh, and one thing, General. There's no such thing as a black tulip.
Lambert What?
Thurloe There is nothing black in nature. If you look carefully you'll find it's dark purple.
Lambert Is there nothing your spies don't tell you?
Thurloe Very little.

Marvell enters, shabbily dressed, nervous

Marvell Oh, I beg pardon. The Protector wishes to see me.
Lambert Wait in the gallery.
Marvell I have been. For three days. It's so crammed with Parliament men there's nowhere to sit. And the rain's coming in. But I shall return there. (*He starts to leave*)
Thurloe No, stay. His Highness wishes to talk to you particularly.
Lambert I'd better go and see if he's all right. He can't have fallen through the floor yet. Can he?

Lambert exits

Thurloe shuffles his papers

Thurloe What's it about?
Marvell Assistant Latin Secretary.
Thurloe Ah yes. You wrote "The Protector's First Anniversary" for us?

Marvell nods cautiously

We thought it spoke well for the government.
Marvell Thank you.
Thurloe Right. John Milton needs an assistant. I'm doing half his work for him — council minutes, foreign correspondence.
Marvell His eyesight …
Thurloe Yes, yes, we know. We've reduced his salary by fifty pounds. Not that that would come to you, mind. (*Finding a paper*) Now, Milton speaks highly of your Latin.
Marvell I'm obliged.
Thurloe What other languages do you have? Living, preferably.
Marvell French, Italian — Spanish, Dutch.
Thurloe Swedish?
Marvell No.
Thurloe (*making a note*) No Swedish. We liked the "First Anniversary". The Protector was much taken with the line, "If these the times, then this should be the man."

Marvell Must. "This *must* be the man." Tee, tee, em, em.

Thurloe (*uncomprehendingly*) Yes … but it's the "Horatian Ode" that sticks. It circulated much among royalists.

Marvell I had no hand in that.

Thurloe Nevertheless. And you continued to travel abroad throughout the war?

Marvell I was completing my education.

Thurloe Like so many men who dodged the war. England should be the most educated nation on Earth. Instead of which Milton is the only man in Whitehall who can write a letter in decent Latin. And since he imagines Cicero reads them personally, he composes about one a month. It's no way to conduct a foreign policy.

Marvell No. If Mr Milton would allow me …

Cromwell enters

Cromwell My ceiling's on the shitting floor now, plaster everywhere … Who are you?

Thurloe Mr Marvell.

Cromwell "Horatian Ode" Marvell?

Marvell Yes … Your Majesty——

Thurloe Highness. Majesty is for kings. I have it here. (*He hands four handwritten sheets to Cromwell*)

Cromwell Though I doubt Horace ever wrote anything so damned obscure. Thurloe, I need something to eat. Cold mutton, a pie, anything.

Thurloe You are supposed to be eating only fish and vegetables.

Cromwell Vegetables! Melancholy and wind. Fish — find me some oysters then.

Thurloe I doubt your lady would count oysters as fish …

Cromwell Out!

Thurloe exits with dignity

You want Milton's job?

Marvell No, no. I wish to assist him. Lighten his load.

Cromwell He doesn't seem very laden to me.

Marvell His health has been imperfect …

Cromwell So he tells us. Yet he's married again, and his wife is with child. I would say he shows signs of recovery. Praise be.

Marvell Praise be.

Cromwell Thurloe tells me when foreigners come to London, they wish to gawp at two men only — myself and Milton. But I sit here, a prisoner in this great warren, while the world flocks to his cottage. They sit and boggle at the great mind and drink five bottles of wine apiece.

Marvell Five!

Cromwell How do I know? Because — and here's the rub — I agreed to pay his table bills. Don't think I'd do the same for his assistant. Every poet in England would be drinking at my expense. (*He picks up the pages*) You wrote this?

Marvell Er?

Cromwell "An Horatian Ode upon Cromwell's Return from Ireland." Seven years ago.

Marvell I did, Your — Highness. I never intended to publish it.

Cromwell Your hand?

Marvell I believe so, but ——

Cromwell Well then. "So restless Cromwell could not cease / In the inglorious arts of peace." Inglorious?

Marvell (*hesitantly*) We live in a world, alas, where no glory attaches to peace. Whereas it should be the triumph of your reign — your rule. It's ironic.

Cromwell Ah. Irony. Led some men to the scaffold. Page two — you get even more obscure. Before the war, you say, I lived "reserved and austere / As if my higher plot / Was to plant the bergamot." The bergamot being?

Marvell The king of pears.

Cromwell *King* of pears? Perhaps not such a forced rhyme?

Marvell Your Highness sees connections that had escaped me.

Cromwell Surely not? Irony. No bergamot in the Fens however. Where are you from?

Marvell Hull. Very little bergamot round Hull.

Cromwell Wouldn't flavour the herrings. Loyal town though.

Marvell I hope to stand for Parliament there one day.

Cromwell Do you now? A Yorkshire poet in the Commons. One less lawyer, I suppose. Sit down, man. Have you eaten?

Marvell (*eagerly*) No.

Cromwell Good. Neither have I. Let's come to the king. Charles, "the royal actor born". Why so?

Marvell Charles was born to be king. Born, that is, to be an actor in history. The role was forced upon him.

Cromwell And Cromwell? Is he too an actor born?

Beat

Marvell Providence has given you a role to play.

Cromwell But not from birth?

Marvell I believe God saw that Charles must be overthrown — by force … And he chose you to be an instrument of that force.

Cromwell I enter merely to overthrow the king. In Act Five?

Lambert Not merely, no. I believe you were chosen for greater tasks.
Cromwell Namely?
Marvell To bring harmony and settlement to a land torn by civil war ... to
defeat the Antichrist both at home and abroad ... to be our Moses and lead
us to the promised land.
Cromwell Really. I feel that deserves a whole new play. Part Two perhaps?
Marvell Your Highness plainly understands the conventions of drama.

Beat

Cromwell The king
                    "Nothing common did or mean
                    Upon that memorable scene:
                    But with his keener eye
                    The axe's edge did try:
                    Nor called the gods with vulgar spite
                    To vindicate his hapless right,
                    But bowed his comely head
                    Down, as upon a bed."
I didn't see it. I was at prayer with my officers. Where were you, Marvell?

Marvell is silent

Did you see the execution?

Beat

Marvell Yes.
Cromwell Why?
Marvell I was in London. It seemed to me — that after "that memorable
hour" nothing in the world would ever be the same.
Cromwell The passing of an age?
Marvell More. The breaking of myth and ritual.
Cromwell You mourn their end?
Marvell The king's world was doomed. But the passing of a thousand years
of monarchy should not go unremarked. However great its successor.
Cromwell None of your lick-arsing, man. I've read your latest stuff. I am "a
star", "heaven's favourite", "angelic Cromwell who outwings the wind".
I get this turd by the yardful from Dryden and Waller.
Marvell Yes, but Dryden doesn't understand tetrameters, and Waller's
rhymes merely tinkle ...

Thurloe enters with a tray of food and drink

Thurloe No oysters, Your Highness, but some fresh turbot.

Cromwell Put it down, put it down.

Thurloe There are many — *important* people anxious to see you. The delegation has had no food …

Cromwell Give them my vegetables then. This *(waving the poem)* is more important. Any news of Blake?

Thurloe None.

Cromwell He may be buried at sea by now. Vegetables!

Thurloe takes the vegetables and scowls a reproach at Marvell. Cromwell sits, takes a bite of bread, after holding the fish up and disdaining it, and pours himself some ale. Marvell looks on miserably

I am "the force of angry heaven's flame". So the Lord is on my side?

Marvell No man is more blessed.

Cromwell Yet I have "ruined the great work of time". I have destroyed the "great" institution of monarchy?

Marvell *(reluctantly)* Yes.

Cromwell   "Through justice against fate complain
                  And plead the ancient rights in vain."
How can God's providence be opposed to earthly justice?

Marvell I don't know.

Cromwell What do you mean — you don't know? It's impossible — the two must be in harmony.

Marvell Providence dictated Richard II should lose his crown, but Bolingbroke could claim no legal right in seizing it.

Cromwell Have a care, Marvell …

Marvell It seems to me that God subjects mankind to plague and famine, tempest and earthquake …

Cromwell Ay.

Marvell So he subjects the governments of the world to seasons of discord and war.

Cromwell Then he has a purpose.

Marvell He must. But we cannot always understand his purpose.

Cromwell Because our minds are feeble.

Marvell The Black Death killed half Europe. Children died in unspeakable pain. What was the purpose of that?

Cromwell is silent

Milton believes Providence demonstrates God's mercy and benevolence. We all want that to be true. But I cannot see it.

Cromwell Go on, man, go on. Eat. Drink. (*He thrusts food at Marvell*) God is on my side, but justice and right are on the Stuarts. How? How?

Marvell (*munching bread*) I believe — that two rights, two forms of goodness may collide, and that it is in the nature of the world that one good may destroy another. As gardens do wild flowers.

Cromwell But everything about me here is force, destruction, power — everything but goodness.

Marvell (*gulping ale and getting carried away*) You came to power by the sword — that is not to be denied. Charles was given no fair trial, however right the verdict. But Providence has made you legitimate.

Cromwell But in English law I'm still a usurper who rules only by force? I am a Bolingbroke, to be racked with guilt all my life? And Charles was not a tyrant who spilled innocent blood? He was a Richard II, to be made a saint?

Marvell Charles was indeed a tyrant ...

Cromwell But we were wrong to depose him?

Marvell I believe when a government is corrupt, the people are forced to take back the sovereignty they have delegated. By rebellion if necessary.

Cromwell Good, good.

Marvell And you made that possible. No-one else could have done it. But men died, the saints did not prevail, Christ did not come down among us.

Cromwell We await him daily.

Marvell Amen.

Cromwell You scribblers are all the same. Utopia without bloodshed.

Marvell I raise my glass. (*He does so*) But I know it's not possible. We all have a notion of an ideal government, an ideal ruler, an ideal state of existence ...

Cromwell Indeed.

Marvell But between the world we long for and the world we inhabit is a mighty chasm. And since the world will not be better, we must stand ever on our guard.

Cromwell Even a poet?

Marvell I find my solitude — delicious. I'd prefer to lie still in some secret nest and keep my silent judgement. But I know a good cause signifies little unless is well defended. Ancient rights hold or break as men are strong and weak.

Cromwell And I am the destroyer of ancient rights ...

Marvell That I never ——

Cromwell (*thumping the paper*) It is here, Marvell — "justice pleads the ancient rights in vain".

Marvell Yes, but that is the past. The future is yours.

Cromwell Mine? I'll be dead soon.

Marvell Then those who inherit your world.

Cromwell I wouldn't put too much faith in them.

Beat

You seek a post in government?
Marvell I do, Your Highness.
Cromwell Why?
Marvell I fear I may remain a tutor forever.
Cromwell So your pen is for hire?
Marvell No.
Cromwell How so?
Marvell A writer is not to sell his voice to one side or the other, but to fight the cause of virtue — however forsaken. To remind men that good is good, however wretched it may appear, and crimes are crimes, however successful they be.

Cromwell stares at him, uncertain how barbed this is

Cromwell Wait in the gallery.
Marvell (*hurriedly putting down his food*) Your Highness.
Cromwell Take your food.

Marvell takes some bread, but Cromwell grabs it and thrusts the turbot into his hands instead

Marvell exits

(*Calling*) Hingston, play me something. You choose. English.

Hingston starts a fantasia by Byrd

William Byrd. Sublime. Another secret papist, mind. (*He picks up the "Horatian Ode"*)
>   "Could by industrious valour climb
>   To ruin the great work of time,
>   And cast the kingdom old
>   Into another mould.
>   Through justice against fate complain
>   And plead the ancient rights in vain."

Damn ancient rights! Damn the great work of time! Oh, God forgive me.

Bettie bursts in

Bettie Does he get the job?

Cromwell Who?
Bettie Mr Marvell.

She tugs Marvell through the door into sight

Cromwell Not suited to government.
Bettie But he's going to write a masque for Fanny's wedding.
Cromwell Wedding?
Bettie To Robert Rich. Oh, Father, you know you will give in at the end. Andrew is writing a masque about Cynthia and Endymion, and Mr Lawes is setting it to music, and Fanny and Robert will sing, and you, Father, if you are very agreeable about the wedding, are to be given a part too.

Cromwell is about to protest

No, not a singing part — I've stood next to you in church. A speaking part. You are to play Jove.

Thurloe enters unobtrusively, carrying a bag

And then if you consent to be the king, you may wear the crown.
Cromwell (*to Thurloe*) Am I the last person in Whitehall to know all this?
Thurloe Lady Elizabeth has been making plans in the event of her sister marrying.
Cromwell So you're in it as well.
Bettie Of course Thurloe's in it. How could Mr Hingston hire fifty violins in London without Thurloe knowing?

Hingston's Byrd shudders to a halt

Oh, sorry, Mr Hingston …
Cromwell Fifty violins!
Bettie I know, it was difficult. It'll be easier when you set up their college.
Cromwell College?
Thurloe Your Highness agreed to set up a Committee for the Advancement of Music.
Cromwell A committee, not a college.
Bettie Committees always lead to colleges.
Cromwell (*groaning*) Colleges always lead to New Music. There is to be no wedding to Robert Rich.
Bettie But Father ——
Cromwell No wedding.

Lambert strides in, followed by Frances

Lambert Why have you countermanded my orders? We haven't even had the panelling out yet.

Cromwell I'm not spending another night here. If I'm to be blown up, I want to be in my own bed.

Lambert is about to argue, but Frances intervenes

Frances Quite right, Your Highness. This is no place to find you.

Bettie Though some found you at the crack of dawn. (*An inclination*) Lady Lambert.

Frances (*curtsying*) Lady Elizabeth.

Bettie Did your ladyship enjoy the opera yesterday?

Frances I beg pardon.

Bettie The opera?

Frances Ah. You were there yourself perhaps?

Bettie Hardly, Lady Lambert. Thurloe saw you.

Cromwell Opera? What is op-e-ra? Not "works" surely?

Thurloe A form of masque, Your Highness.

Bettie The music plays all the time, and the words are all sung, and the story is true history.

Cromwell Terrible hotchpotch. Neither one thing or the other. Who thought of it?

Frances Monteverdi wrote some successful ——

Cromwell Ah! I might have known. New Music!

Thurloe Not necessarily, Your Highness ——

Cromwell What were you doing there, Thurloe?

Thurloe No-one else was free.

Cromwell Free?

Thurloe To note down royalists present.

Cromwell Hm. Is the whole of Whitehall to spend its afternoons at the opera now? Where will all that end?

Lambert Like all fashions it will pass.

Cromwell Hm. Who devised this "opera"?

Frances Sir William Davenant.

Cromwell Davenant! I let him out of prison, and now he's setting up theatres again — contrary to Parliament's decree.

Lambert I'll close it down tomorrow.

Frances You will not.

Lambert Theatres are centres of sedition. Allow a thousand people to assemble under one roof, and there's no knowing what they may devise.

Frances Like churches.

Lambert No, unlike the scriptures plays are lewd and immoral, and their message invariably anti-government.

Thurloe But opera isn't theatre. Plays, I grant you, are filthy and obscene, but opera is different ...

Bettie The characters represent only valour and conjugal love.

Thurloe The good triumph, and the bad go mad.

Cromwell I like the sound of that.

Thurloe You would indeed, Your Highness. And the sight. *The Siege of Rhodes.*

Cromwell (*interested*) Siege of where?

Thurloe Rhodes, Your Highness. It's near Greece. It's the title of Davenant's opera.

Bettie It has sliding scenery — the fleet of Solyman the Magnificent and his army, and the island of Rhodes, and the siege of the city ...

Cromwell You've not seen it yourself?

Bettie I heard about it — from Mr Marvell.

Marvell Erm ...

Bettie Davenant's asked him to write an opera.

Cromwell Has he?

Marvell Not for a theatre, Your Highness. Sir William presents his operas at Rutland House, in the courtyard. The stage is — the size of this room.

Cromwell Can't get much of Solyman's army on it then?

Marvell No, but — Davenant is such a masterly producer ...

Frances He's said to be Shakespeare's natural son.

Cromwell Shakespeare! Another royalist. Eh, Marvell?

Marvell He was — a hater of tyranny.

Cromwell And a lover of legitimacy. Like you — sat on the fence. Milton told me the king had Shakespeare's plays beside him when we had him in prison, kept thinking up new titles for them. If Charles had only studied scripture half as much as Shakespeare and Jonson, he might have kept his head.

Marvell I don't believe we can blame the fall of monarchy solely on Shakespeare, Your Highness. He was a great authority on the hypocrisy of kings.

Bettie signals for Marvell to stop, but he is oblivious

His *Richard III* shows how predictably pious words issue from the mouths of tyrants.

Thurloe joins in the signals

Also *Titus Andronicus.*

A general wince

Cromwell Never heard of it.
Marvell Well, it's not a specially puritan work. But it is plain in *Julius Caesar* ——

A bigger wince

—— where Caesar is offered the … (*He trails off at last*)
Cromwell Well, what about *Julius Caesar*?
Marvell (*cautiously*) It contains many justifications for rebellion …
Cromwell Caesar is offered the crown three times, and is then murdered.
"The world is furnished well with me,
And men are flesh and blood, and apprehensive;
Yet in the number I do know but one
That unassailable hold on his rank,
Unshaked of motion; and I am he."
(*He looks challengingly round the room*) And then they kill him.

A difficult silence

Marvell (*apparently unperturbed*) True, but Brutus was an honourable man, and Shakespeare has written ——
Thurloe An unsatisfactory play. And not one that will ever make an opera.
Frances Your Highness would have enjoyed the singing. Mr Cook as Solyman …
Bettie A bit flat. But Mrs Coleman as Ianthe …
Cromwell *Mrs* Coleman?

Another difficult silence

Thurloe Mr Coleman sang ——
Cromwell Bettie clearly said *Mrs* Coleman. (*Sarcastically*) Even though she was not present herself.
Bettie Yes … Mrs Coleman is married.
Thurloe To Mr Coleman.
Cromwell No woman has ever appeared on an English stage.
Lambert And never will.
Frances But there was no impropriety. Mr and Mrs Coleman sang together. They are married.
Thurloe To each other.
Frances They faced the audience. Not one another.
Bettie They didn't act. No-one acted. It was opera.
Cromwell Opera! Foreign plots, sliding scenery, singing wives … It's a sink of iniquity.

Bettie These are new times, Father. If you turn the world about, nothing stays the same. Hingston will sound like Monteverdi ...

An answering Italianate trill

Cromwell Over my dead body. D'you hear, Hingston? You're English. Tallis and Byrd and Dowland. I tell you there has been too much overturning in this land. Too little respect for tradition.
Bettie But Davenant has a new idea ——
Cromwell Enough. I have matters to decide with Parliament. Leave us.

General bowing

Bettie and Marvell exit

The Lamberts hover

Frances Perhaps Your Highness might be at liberty later in the day?
Cromwell Perhaps.
Frances I shall remain at court then.

Frances curtsies, shoots a look at Lambert, and they exit

Thurloe shuts and locks the door, and produces his bag. He lifts out a golden orb and sceptre, and a seal. Cromwell picks up the orb in his left hand

Cromwell Damned heavy. Where's the crown?
Thurloe At the goldsmith's. He's trying to make it lighter.
Cromwell Hm. What's this?
Thurloe The great seal.
Cromwell Where's the picture of Parliament?
Thurloe It's been replaced by Your Highness sitting on the throne.
Cromwell That won't do. (*He picks up the sceptre in his right hand*) How do I look?
Thurloe Regal.
Cromwell Hm.
Thurloe The delegation were not pleased with the vegetables.
Cromwell Good.
Thurloe They have new proposals.

Cromwell sits and replaces the orb and sceptre on the table

Cromwell So? What do I have to concede in return for orb and sceptre?

Thurloe A written constitution.

Cromwell No bad thing.

Thurloe You would be advised by a council of twenty-one.

Cromwell Chosen by?

Thurloe Yourself. But approved by Parliament.

Cromwell Parliament would have a veto?

Thurloe It would be negotiated.

Cromwell Ah — more work for lawyers.

Thurloe They have agreed to a second chamber, a senate of between forty and seventy. The Commons needs a check or balancing power.

Cromwell Also elected?

Thurloe No. For if they were of the same composition as the Commons, they would be no check upon them. They must be independent, nominated by yourself but approved by Parliament.

Cromwell Utter confusion.

Thurloe Yes, but there is no sure way of choosing men of independent mind.

Cromwell God will choose.

Thurloe In my experience, Your Highness, God has not yet given his full attention to the election of members of Parliament.

Cromwell No. Titles?

Thurloe No earls and dukes. The House of Lords is dead.

Cromwell Not before time. What about the army?

Thurloe A standing army of thirty thousand ...

Cromwell It gets smaller every day.

Thurloe We have forty-eight thousand men still in arms. They cost two million pounds a year. Civil government only gets three hundred thousand. It's quite out of proportion.

Cromwell How much are the Commons offering us?

Thurloe £1,300,000.

Cromwell Ridiculous.

Thurloe Even with a reduced army we need at least two million.

Cromwell So we borrow.

Thurloe The City certainly won't lend us any more.

Cromwell The people will find the money. They like to see England powerful in Europe.

Thurloe I have never observed the people of England eager to pay for their position in Europe. Quite the contrary. There is only one way — through Parliament. They must be persuaded to grant further taxation.

Cromwell Yes, but in return they'll want to control everything — the council, the army, the senate — your spies, Milton's wine bills ... the opera.

Thurloe Sharing of power must be the basis of any settlement.

Cromwell (*jumping up and pacing*) Settlement! God knows I love that word. England has never needed it more. The war was never the end of our labours, but the means — the means by which this nation might be settled on the basis of God and our liberties.

Thurloe Amen to that.

Cromwell But these endless constitutions will never be a solution without the goodwill of the people. Thurloe, what is the true end of government?

Thurloe That the nation will be secure.

Cromwell And what shall make it secure? That the goodness of every citizen shall thrive and multiply — be they Christian, Jew, or Mohammedan. This nation's future depends upon reformation — the mind is the man. I tell you I am not wedded or glued to *forms* of government. They are dross and dung when compared with Christ. What forms of government can ensure a sinless society?

Thurloe None. But what church preaches to a sinless congregation? Don't, whatever you do, put your trust in the goodness of the people.

Cromwell Ay, that I've learned. The people should have what's for their good, not what pleases them. But how can we trust Parliament's law? They change it monthly according to their whim.

Thurloe But you cannot rule without Parliament.

Cromwell Thurloe, I sat on the back benches of the Commons for years. I know its very taste and smell. And I will support it till my dying day. But why, Thurloe, why do they elect such imbeciles? Can this be the best that England has to offer? Feudal die-hards, apeish courtiers, religious bigots? Farmers and merchants, who have no interest but their own, who hold that little government is good government, that what is right for Guildford must be right for England.

Thurloe If you dispose of Parliament, it is against the will of the nation. There will be nine in ten against you.

Cromwell But what if I disarm the nine and put a sword in the tenth man's hand? That would do the business.

Beat

Thurloe Your Highness knows he has no need to rule by the sword. Your authority is unassailable, with or without the army. The great question is — how is this authority to outlive you? There are men waiting for you to die to break the nation apart, smother democracy, destroy religious liberty, surrender our power abroad. Even restore the Stuarts.

Cromwell Don't worry, Thurloe, you'll be safe enough. You know too much about everyone — including Charles Stuart.

Thurloe If the Stuarts return, there won't be any more Thurloes. A man as poor as I will never hold high office again. The rich and the highborn will control every office of state — king, Parliament, law, church, army.

Cromwell (*sarcastically*) Making me King will save the republic?

Thurloe If you will. We've splintered the country into a thousand factions. Everything has turned upside down. A radical like Sexby should be fighting to save the republic. But what's he doing instead? Taking money from the Stuarts to kill you and put them back on the throne. He may be mad, but he does recognize that England will unite behind one thing only — the office of king. The king may no longer be God's anointed, but at least he stops generals and demagogues filling his place.

Cromwell I see. I'm to fill a place. Back to the old ways.

Thurloe No, forward to the new. A single ruler, restrained by a nominated council and an elected Parliament. Revolution and tradition entwined. The English way — harmony in confusion. Make Richard your successor. He's no Protector, but the *office* of King will carry him through. And the House of Cromwell shall rule for a thousand years.

Cromwell is silent

I sense Your Highness is out of mind.

Cromwell I see it is the best way forward.

Thurloe Then what is the obstacle?

Cromwell The title of King.

Thurloe Ah. I have thought long about this. If the name is the problem, then I believe Parliament would accept the proposal that you take the title of — Emperor.

Cromwell Emperor?

Thurloe Yes. Oliver, Emperor of Great Britain.

Cromwell ponders this, as the Lights fade. The storm continues

CURTAIN

ACT II

The same. Two hours later

The storm continues

Cromwell enters

Cromwell King of Britain ... Emperor of Great Britain. King of England, Scotland and Ireland, Emperor of England, Scotland, Wales ...

Hingston. "Can she excuse my wrongs"! My wife sings it. Dowland. Incomparable. Another papist.

Hingston starts to play

(*Singing along*) "Càn she excuse my wrongs ..." (*Speaking*)Too high for me. Terrible dinner. Mackerel! Carrots and peas. If I find the delegation got meat ... And still raining. The palace will be afloat soon.

No news from Blake. The Spanish fleet must be entering Cadiz by now. That means a million pounds for the Inquisition, fifty thousand soldiers to invade Ireland. Blake's even older than me. We can't be back and forth across the Atlantic at our age.

But at least he's out there fighting a war. He's not a prisoner in a palace, chopping logic with lawyers, choosing designs for crown and sceptre. I'd change places with him tomorrow.

"Killing No Murder". (*He takes up the pamphlet; reading*) "Above all, tyrants pretend a love to God and religion. His Highness has found indeed in godliness there is a great gain, and that preaching and praying, well managed, will obtain other kingdoms as well as heaven."

He kneels

Lord, if it be your will that I should take the crown — which I value not a trifle for its own sake — then give me some sign. But if you take me up into a high place but to tempt me — then show me the error of my ways. Lord, do not desert me in my hour of trial. Even for Jesus Christ's sake. Amen.

He listens for a moment, and then sings

> "Better a thousand times to die
> Than for to live thus still tormented."

(*Speaking*) Perhaps Sexby will finish it for me. Under the bed — quick and free of pain. Oh, God forgive me.

Bettie bursts in, followed by Marvell who is carrying papers

Bettie We have come to read you Andrew's new opera. There is a part for you.
Cromwell I thought you had me down as Jove.
Bettie No, no. This is bigger than Jove. You can play yourself.
Cromwell Bettie, I have work to do.
Bettie But you've hardly finished dinner. I hear you ate very little mackerel, and Mother will be angry.
Cromwell Only if someone tells her.

Bettie smiles

Bettie You'll like the part.
Cromwell Too soon after vegetables. Sing to me. "Can she excuse my wrongs".
Bettie Oh not "Better a thousand times to die". I'm about to give birth, not expire. No, Mr Hingston and I have been practising something.

Hingston plays the intro to "Gather ye Rosebuds". Cromwell groans

Richard enters and stands in the doorway

Now behave, Father. Keep still, Dick. Not too fast, Mr Hingston. (*She sings*)

Gather ye Rosebuds

> "Gather ye rosebuds while ye may,
> Old Time is still a-flying:
> And this same flower that smiles today
> Tomorrow will be dying.
>
> The glorious lamp of heaven, the sun,
> The higher he's a-getting,
> The sooner will his race be run,
> And nearer he's to setting.

That age is best which is the first,
When youth and blood are warmer;
But being spent, the worse, and worst
Times still succeed the former.

Then be not coy, but use your time,
And while ye may, go marry:
For having lost but once your prime,
You may for ever tarry."

Silence for a moment

Bettie It can't have been that bad.
Cromwell It was beautiful.
Richard Yes, it was.
Marvell Huzzah, Lady Elizabeth. (*He starts to clap, glances at Cromwell and stops*)
Bettie (*curtsying, beaming*) Thank you, thank you. Thank you, Mr Hingston.
Cromwell Herrick. Is he to your taste then, Marvell?
Marvell I — admire parts of Herrick.
Cromwell Always on about some mistress or other. Is that one of your pleasures?
Marvell I am not as easily bewitched by petticoats as Herrick. He seems to fear only his breath stealing from him, while I sense before me deserts of vast eternity.
Cromwell Eternity is a state to be desired. Do you not accept God's providence?
Marvell I believe … in a necessity that is pre-eternal to all things.
Richard That means no freedom at all.
Marvell Freedom … is the knowledge of necessity.
Cromwell Amen.
Marvell Once we accept that all things happen in their best and proper time, we are free. Wisdom is to make our destiny our choice.
Cromwell A wisdom beyond the reach of most of us.
Marvell Naturally. We all yearn after a wholeness that is unattainable. Our burden is to adjust to our fallen state — and all our life we rage against the task.

Beat

Bettie Too much, too much. Andrew and I came here to discuss his opera. (*Calling*) Thurloe! You can run the country for ten minutes.

Thurloe enters immediately

Thurloe A rash command, Lady Elizabeth. I could change much in ten minutes.

Cromwell Nonsense, Thurloe. You've run the country for days on end.

Thurloe (*producing papers*) There are papers to sign, Your Highness. Urgently.

Cromwell I prefer even opera to papers.

Thurloe (*after a glare at Marvell*) I shall go and make the most of my ten minutes.

Thurloe exits, leaving papers on the table

Bettie Andrew, explain to Father.

Cromwell looks witheringly at Marvell

Marvell (*hesitantly*) Sir William Davenant had two ideas for his next opera. One on Sir Francis Drake ——

Bettie You've always admired Drake, Father.

Cromwell Drake was a plain, blunt speaker. I can't hear him trilling up and down to Monteverdi. What's the other idea?

Marvell The other concerns — Spain.

Cromwell Spain!

Bettie Wait, Father ——

Cromwell I'll have nothing Spanish in my court.

Bettie Listen, Father. Andrew has a petition from Davenant.

Marvell May I read it, Your Highness?

Cromwell Be brief.

Marvell (*reading*) "The people of England are observed by all nations to require continual diversions, being otherwise naturally inclined to that melancholy that breeds sedition ——"

Cromwell True enough.

Marvell (*reading*) "— which made our ancestors entertain them with public meetings for prizes in archery, horse races, maypoles, matches at football, and theatres."

Cromwell The English need fasting and prayer, not theatres and football. Where does Spain come in?

Marvell (*reading*) "If moral representations may be allowed — being without obscenity and scandal — the first subject might consist of the Spaniard's barbarous conquests in the Americas and of their cruelties exercised upon the subjects of those nations."

Bettie The title of the opera is *The Cruelty of the Spaniards in Peru.*

Cromwell Promising. Strange subject to set to music.

Marvell Mr Milton liked it. He told me to study your speeches to Parliament.

Cromwell Did he now?

Marvell He pointed out that when you declared war on Spain two years ago, you said it was to "avenge the blood of the poor Indians, which had been so cruelly shed by the Spaniards".

Cromwell That — and other reasons.

Richard Colonies, booty.

Marvell But I was struck by what followed. "Since God has made of one blood all nations of men, all wrongs down to particular persons ought to be considered as done to the rest of the human race."

Richard The rest of the human race!

Cromwell I'm not surprised Milton pointed that out. He wrote it.

Richard At your orders.

Cromwell I nearly had a seizure when I read it out, I can tell you. God might want me to avenge the downtrodden of the world. But I'd need a thousand ships and a million soldiers.

Richard Your friend Blake sailed into Cadiz in '49, and proclaimed the end of tyranny and the destruction of all monarchs.

Cromwell Ay, we thought that was God's will once …But how can I free all people oppressed by tyranny?

Marvell Who is to decide what is tyranny?

Richard And will such people thank you for it?

Cromwell Ay, and will parliament vote me a hundred million pounds?

Richard If their property was at stake they would. Look what they voted to defeat the Irish — high among the downtrodden of the world.

Cromwell The Irish …

Bettie Don't get Father on to Ireland …

Cromwell When Spain invades us again, it'll be through Ireland.

Richard Spain! Father, you're obsessed with armadas and popes and Jesuits and inquisitions and Spanish treasure fleets. You're still living in the reign of Elizabeth and waiting for the Armada.

Cromwell The Roman Antichrist is our sworn enemy and Spain is his lieutenant.

Richard Father!

Cromwell Spain is a dark empire, out to dominate the world, enslave the Americas, and rule men's minds through torture and the inquisition.

Marvell That's why we thought an opera on the subject might … help.

Bettie We could call it *The Dark Empire*.

Cromwell No, I like *The Cruelty of the Spaniards*. Leaves no room for doubt.

Marvell It would educate parliament in the evils of Spanish domination.

Bettie Since all Whitehall wants to go to the opera.

Cromwell Ay. Ay, it might. Music has the power to stir men's souls.

Bettie A private performance for them — in the Banqueting Hall perhaps?

Cromwell It must have tunes.

Bettie Certainly.

Cromwell And no female singers. Not even Mrs ——

Marvell Coleman.

Cromwell I know Parliament men. Too easily distracted from the root of the matter by a skirt and an ankle.

Bettie The female characters will have to wear skirts.

Cromwell Ay, but we'll know they're boys. So, no distraction there.

Marvell Oh, none.

Richard Poor Mrs Coleman. The last female opera singer.

Cromwell Why are there females anyway?

Bettie Perhaps Peruvians wanted children.

Cromwell Yes, yes, but women play no part in the story.

Richard Except to get killed.

Bettie Father you have to have a love story.

Cromwell Why?

Bettie People won't go to an opera without one. Even Shakespeare puts in a love story.

Cromwell Not in *Julius Caesar*. What's your plot, Marvell?

Marvell There's Pizarro the Spanish general, and his chaplain Las Casas and Atabaliba the Emperor of Peru.

Bettie Atabaliba has a daughter called Amaru, and there's a young Spanish lieutenant called Martinez.

Cromwell They fall in love.

Marvell Your Highness is very quick.

Cromwell It's not the most novel of plots.

Marvell No. In Scene One Martinez thanks God for the paradise that is America.

Cromwell Good. Well, let's hear it.

Marvell Thank you, Your Highness.

> "What should we do but sing His praise
> That led us through the watery maze
> Unto a land so long unknown
> And yet far kinder than our own,
> Where He the huge sea-monsters wracks
> That lift the deep upon their backs,
> He lands us on a grassy stage
> Safe from the storms, and prelate's rage ..."

Cromwell Good. More.

Marvell
> "He gave us this eternal spring
> Which here enamels everything
> He hangs in shades the orange bright
> Like golden lamps in a green night,
> He makes the figs our mouths to meet

> And throws the melons at our feet;
> But apples plants of such a price
> No tree could ever bear them twice."

Cromwell Apples in Peru? Are you sure?

Marvell I made it up.

Cromwell Huh. Still, I like it so far.

Marvell Thank you, Your Highness. Martinez is captured by the Peruvians.

Bettie And then captivated by Amaru.

Marvell In Act Two Pizzaro takes Atabaliba prisoner, forces him to pay a huge ransom, but still decides to kill him.

Cromwell Perfidious Spain. Good, good.

Marvell And then there's a heavenly intervention. I thought perhaps Your Highness might appear — in a vision.

Cromwell A vision? Sounds Papist to me.

Marvell We can make it a very Puritan vision.

Cromwell No descent from on high?

Marvell No, no. You could just — walk on.

Cromwell No smoke, no bells?

Marvell Definitely not. But a slight roll on the drums perhaps?

Cromwell Drums I like. Even cymbals.

Marvell A clash of cymbals, good, and then you have this speech.

Cromwell As Lord Protector?

Marvell Yes.

Cromwell I would act me?

Marvell Yes. Davenant wants an English army to arrive, led of course by you.

Cromwell I've never set foot in Peru.

Bettie It's not real. It's an opera.

Marvell Theatre is not bound by time and place, Your Highness.

Cromwell Then theatre is a liar.

Bettie You'll like the speech, Father. Andrew wrote it specially for you.

She hands Cromwell the speech. He eyes it dubiously

From "What is the duty of the strong".

Cromwell (*reading reluctantly*)
> "What is the duty of the strong, but break
> The oppressor in pieces, release all slaves
> From tyranny, relieve the poor with bread."

Sounds like Milton at his most airy.

Bettie Do go on — and don't mumble. A little more fervour.

Cromwell (*reading loudly*)
> "For wrongs done any of God's creatures
> Are wrongs done the rest of the human race."

Bettie That was more ordering the infantry to wheel right — but it was better.
Cromwell (*reading quieter*)
>   "So England speaks for people everywhere
>   Against the wolfish foes of liberty" ——

I've told you, we can't afford it.
Bettie Please, Father.
Cromwell (*reading*)
>   "Against the wolfish foes of liberty,
>   Among whose number Spain must be the first."

That I like.
Bettie There's more to come.
Cromwell (*reading*)
>   "The far Americas have bred a race,
>   Simple, faithful, pure in mind" ——

Only four beats to that line.
Bettie I beg your pardon.
Cromwell "*Sim*ple, *faith*ful, *pure* in *mind*." Only four beats. I was trained in mathematics.
Bettie (*sotto*) Clearly not in poetry.
Marvell (*hastily*) Your Highness is entirely right. I sometimes use four beats for added emphasis.
Cromwell Nonsense. Just laziness.
Marvell I shall of course rewrite the line.
Cromwell Good. (*Reading*)
>   "Simple, faithful, pure in mind DE DUM,
>   In one thing only are they bless'd and curs'd —
>   Silver and gold grow like orchards in the sun
>   And tempt the avarice of visiting man."

Every Spanish treasure fleet we've seized has been a blessing to us, not a curse. If Blake hasn't captured their latest one, I can't pay the army.
Bettie Oh, do go on.
Cromwell (*reading*)
>   "Upon these gentle lambs you Spanish fell
>   Like ravening wolves upon the innocent fold."

"Ravening wolves" I like.
Marvell Thank you.
Cromwell Not original, of course.
Marvell No. I think the next lines are.
Cromwell (*reading*)
>   "Ever since the first brother sacrificed
>   The other to revenge; slaughter and war
>   Have made up half the business of the world."

That's well phrased.
Marvell Thank you. You end ——

Cromwell (*reading*)
>   "Yet never was there so arrant a piece
>   Of loathed, dark and bestial tyranny
>   As the cruelty of Spaniards in far Peru."

Final couplet should rhyme.

Marvell Not much rhymes with Peru.

Cromwell True, who, do, Montagu.

Marvell I had forgot Your Highness's gift for rhyme.

Cromwell Does Davenant like all this?

Marvell He — he finds it rather political. Not enough dancing.

Richard Dancing?

Marvell He wants a dance — of apes and baboons.

Cromwell Baboons?

Marvell There is only one baboon. He swings down from a tree, and has a
little dance with the apes. It's not a real baboon, just a child in a baboon
costume …

Cromwell I am not appearing with an infant baboon.

Marvell No, Your Highness.

Cromwell But I think Parliament should hear it. I'll make it all scan first.

Marvell I shall be greatly indebted, Your Highness.

Bettie Why won't you do it, Father? You're acting yourself.

Cromwell It's still a pretence.

Richard Acting is always a pretence of some sort.

Cromwell That's why I hate acting.

Bettie You are a great actor, Father.

Cromwell I hope not, child. (*To Marvell*) Even if Providence would have
me play a role.

Marvell Your Highness.

Cromwell What role does the Almighty have in mind now, do you think,
Marvell?

Beat

Marvell Your Highness chid me once for using irony. I find the Almighty's
ways so unfathomable — that I take him to be the Ironist Supreme.

Cromwell Speak plain, Marvell. Would you have me accept the crown?

Marvell I would the question were so simple.

Cromwell It is simple, man. Yes or no.

Marvell Your Highness, I see a paradox. A man who won't take sides is
incomplete, but as soon as a man does he becomes a fool. So I am on the
rack. Both action and contemplation, in our fallen world, appear to me
immoral.

Cromwell Action is immoral? And you seek a job in government?

Marvell I know that a man may starve at the feast of a good conscience. And yet in my conscience lies the part of me I hold most true.

Cromwell Should I take the crown?

Marvell Abroad Your Highness is already regarded as a king who has hurled the world about him.

Cromwell And at home?

Marvell You have founded a republic and given life back to the nation. You are a prophet armed, our Moses, divinely inspired.

Cromwell Would you see me king? Answer plainly.

Beat

Marvell Then plainly put — I see no future in hereditary monarchy.

Cromwell You cling to the republic?

Marvell Much better breathe free and lively as a republican, than choke in the iron chains of monarchy. How can any nation calling themselves free, suffer anyone to claim hereditary right over them.

Lambert enters abruptly

Lambert Sexby is captured.

Cromwell Sexby — where?

Lambert At Deptford. As he took ship for the Netherlands. Still giving out pamphlets.

Cromwell Where is he now?

Lambert In the palace prison.

Cromwell I shall speak to him.

Lambert Out of the question.

Cromwell I shall speak to him. Bring him here.

Lambert exits, sullenly

Leave me. Dick, stay.

Bettie and Marvell exit

Have you thought it over?

Richard There's nothing to think. I told you how I am.

Cromwell God has a purpose for you.

Richard Yes, but no-one knows what it is.

Cromwell Well, it's plainly not to be a painter.

Richard Oh, plainly.

Cromwell We cannot choose our destiny. You cannot be Rubens, I cannot be Dowland.

Richard Dowland!

Cromwell I'd rather have played upon a pipe, and kept a flock of sheep, than been "His Highness".

Richard You're not addressing Parliament now, Father. Save that for the delegation.

Cromwell It's true. The happiest years I spent were at Huntingdon, when you were all young. I had no thought of war, of revolution, of greatness. I was a farmer and a justice of the peace — no more. I believed old age would bring peace and a seat by the fire. Look at me now! A prisoner in this dismal palace, racked with pain from winter soldiering, near dead before I'm sixty.

Richard And that you'd wish on me? It's not enticing.

Cromwell Providence is speaking ...

Richard Father, I have no talent for leadership. Unlike Henry, unlike my dear dead brothers ——

Cromwell Don't speak of your brothers ...

Richard Why not? All my life Robert and Oliver have cast their shadow over me. You've seen to that.

Cromwell That's a lie ——

Richard No, it isn't. You've never been the same man since they died.

Beat

Cromwell It was a dagger to my heart.

Richard Then why didn't you grieve with us — give us some sign that you cared? Bettie and I wept alone. Mother went about her good works. You plunged back into the war. Providence had spoken. Nothing more to be said.

Cromwell The Lord took them into the happiness we all long for.

Richard Why? Why did he take them? Oliver was your greatest joy.

Cromwell doesn't deny it

So why did a god of charity take him from you? Not in battle, mind, serving the great cause. Smallpox.

Beat

Cromwell Perhaps he is not always a benevolent god.

Richard Father!

Cromwell I thought I would go mad. It's true the war saved me ... order ... prayer ... battle. St Paul was my guide. "Not that I speak in respect of want; for I have learned in whatsoever state I am, therewith to be content. I know both how to be abased, and I know how to abound."

Richard Ay — "abound" is your watchword. Not mine. When Oliver died I was eighteen. Old enough to have fought myself. But I had no stomach for it. And you have never forgiven me.

Cromwell Nonsense.

Richard Never.

Cromwell I have tried.

Richard You've "tried".

Cromwell I persuaded myself it was the Lord's mercy that you should live a retired life in the country. That you at least might be preserved.

Richard And the least was preserved. But not I think to be first.

Cromwell Don't take scripture ——

Richard Why must there be a "first man" once you are gone? We have a republic. What need we His Highness, His Majesty?

Cromwell Because there are bitter choices to be made, and only a leader may make them.

Richard Bitter choices?

Cromwell You will face them one day. Do you govern as though the people were Samaritans or Pharisees, good men or knaves?

Richard If men, and women, are given the chance to live in a free republic — in time their natural goodness will shine forth.

Cromwell I thought so once. And I gave them that freedom — and I was answered by ingratitude and self. The English no sooner receive a liberty than they deny it to others. Oh, they show a mighty appetite for spite — to be wounding one another — grovelling and rending and tearing ... I had such hopes, Richard. That I should be a second Solomon. I asked the Lord to give me an understanding heart to judge the people, to discern between good and bad. And I hoped that God would say because I had not asked for riches or long life, that he would give me right judgement.

Richard And the Lord did ...

Cromwell Then why are the people ready to cut one another's throats? Why is the army the only thing that stands between this republic and chaos? Why does Parliament want a king, not a republic? If men are selfish and violent, why is it only a king can save them from destroying themselves?

Richard That is a counsel of despair.

Cromwell It's the only way to save what's left of the revolution. I must be king, and you will be my heir.

Richard Nominate Lambert. Nominate any of your generals ...

Cromwell England doesn't want a nominated monarchy. They don't want a royal family to be *chosen*. They want a royal family thrust upon 'em.

Richard Any royal family?

Cromwell More or less.

Richard It's true — they've endured some terrible monarchs in the name of legitimacy.

Cromwell And they'll continue to …
Richard Thank you, Father.

Cromwell smiles

Cromwell Think upon it, Richard. We do well to make our destiny our choice.

Thurloe enters

Thurloe Your Highness, Sexby is not to be found. General Lambert believes he's been taken to the Tower.
Cromwell You mean Lambert wants him in the Tower. Dick, go and find him, he can't have got far in this storm.
Richard I don't see Lord Johnny allowing me ——
Cromwell Do I have to do everything myself?

Thurloe protests

Cromwell strides out, despite the protests

Thurloe Are you persuaded?
Richard To what?
Thurloe To succeed your father as king.
Richard You think he is decided?
Thurloe Why do you doubt that?
Richard Because all my life I've seen Father leave one person with one notion of his plans …
Thurloe And another with another. It's the art of politics. When you're slow to make up your mind, it pays to keep everyone confident you're leaning their way. But yes, I think he is decided. There's no other choice.
Richard He could stay Protector.
Thurloe Parliament doesn't want a Protector. His power is too ill defined, too unconstrained. The title was created for your father, and it will die with him. Parliament wants a king, and if they can't have a Cromwell, they'll look to a Stuart.
Richard The Stuarts have no love of Parliament.
Thurloe None. It'll be a return to tyranny.

Beat

Richard As king I would have less power than as a Protector?
Thurloe Certainly.

Richard That's a relief.

Thurloe You'd be bound in by a constitution. With a king everyone knows where they are. Rebellion is treason, property is honoured, laws are legal.

Richard Father doesn't care about legality. He only really wants godly reformation.

Thurloe So he tells me twice a day. But he has no plan, no strategy. He wants a national church that can contain all opinions. But when have the most devout ever wanted a broad church? They can't wait to splinter into smaller and smaller sects. I despise them with all my heart. Richard, accept the crown. Don't let your father waver. If he decides against it, he consigns us to anarchy.

Cromwell enters, sword in hand, holding Sexby by the arm. Sexby has his hands tied, and has been roughed up

Cromwell Out, both of you.

Thurloe You must have an armed guard, Your Highness.

Cromwell I need to talk to Sexby alone. Out.

Thurloe But Your Highness ...

Cromwell And if you tell Lambert, you lose your job.

Thurloe and Richard exit

Sit down.

Cromwell places his sword on the table. They eye one another

Sexby You look old, Cromwell.

Cromwell Malaria from those damned Irish bogs. A stone I can't shift.

Sexby They say you're dying.

Cromwell God will choose the time.

Sexby God has chosen mine.

Cromwell You take too many risks, Sexby.

Sexby I learnt them from a master.

Cromwell We fought together eight long years. When did I ever risk my soldiers?

Sexby Dunbar.

Cromwell The choice was clear — attack or die.

Sexby Oh, things were clear once — when you cut off the king's head, when you gave us a republic. We had hope then — that all men should have work, no poor should starve in the streets ...

Cromwell Ay, ay. I remember nonsense too — that men should have many wives, dine off silver plate, eat beef only ...

Sexby I drink to all three. I drink to our revolution — "the most heroic achievement since the beginning of the world".

Cromwell Leveller cant.

Sexby John Milton. And what happened? You turned on your own soldiers, men who would have given power back to the people. At Ware, at Burford.

Cromwell Five men executed in all. The army came to heel. You weren't even there.

Sexby And you rode on to Oxford — for an honorary degree. Doctor of Hypocrisy.

Beat

Cromwell "Killing No Murder". Why?

Sexby To show you the greatest tyrant in history.

Cromwell You and I fought for the people.

Sexby Tyrants often start out as the people's general. You're a fraud, Cromwell. You'd call on God; weep, howl and repent — even as you smote us under the first rib. You were always fluent at weeping — spongy eyes and a supple conscience. You're so certain you're God's chosen, it justifies anything you do.

Cromwell I had no wish to be Protector.

Sexby And when they crown you they'll have to drag you to the throne.

Cromwell Protector or king, I govern through Parliament.

Sexby A Parliament elected by the wealthy. All men should have a voice in how they are to be governed. Free elections would break you.

Cromwell Free elections would bring anarchy. Five to one in England have no house or land. Give them the vote and they will by law make an equality of all possessions. Property will be destroyed.

Sexby When did God stand up for property? Share it out, so that all may have enough.

Cromwell (*exasperated*) How? How are we to share out our inheritance? If we could leap out of one society straight into another, there would be little dispute. But without war and bloodshed and chaos men will not give away the best part of their possessions.

Sexby Reason tells us preservation lies in working one with another.

Cromwell Reason! Men who call upon reason do generally mean their own. I tell you I have no power to parcel out the earth.

Sexby You have more power than ever king of England did. And what do you do with it — exclude Parliament men you don't like, cut short their sessions, raise taxes without their consent …

Cromwell Because they flouted law …

Sexby Law! When have you ever heeded law? You've packed juries with your supporters, replaced judges you didn't like, openly flouted Magna Carta.

Cromwell (*losing his temper*) Oh, I'm sick of judges for ever pleading Magna Carta. Magna Farta more like. Woe to the land that's ruled by a bench of lawyers!

Sexby You've devastated the Irish and stolen their land.

Cromwell The Irish threatened the very existence of this republic.

Sexby What had we to do in Ireland? In '49 the Council of Officers voted that the army in Ireland should not be used either to destroy the natives or deprive them of their estates. And how did you respond — laid siege to Drogheda and massacred their inhabitants.

Cromwell Drogheda! I tell you Drogheda was justified by the rules of war.

Sexby Perhaps the Irish didn't appreciate war had rules.

Cromwell Aston was the governor at Drogheda, an English royalist, served in Germany and Russia — he knew the rules well enough. I summoned the town, he chose to resist. He knew he could expect no quarter. You remember when Rupert took Bolton in '44 he killed sixteen hundred of our garrison, and he was within his rights.

Sexby But three thousand were slaughtered, many of them townspeople.

Cromwell I ordered those bearing arms to be killed. Only citizens with weapons died, whatever lies royalists now tell.

Sexby You'd always shown mercy before, once a garrison was taken.

Cromwell I tell you our whole expedition was in danger. Word had to go the length of Ireland — no mercy to men with arms. You think I should feel remorse at the slaughter. Ay, I should regret my temper but for one thing. It prevented the effusion of blood for the future. The war was soon over.

Sexby It hasn't brought peace.

Cromwell It will. Not in my lifetime perhaps. But it will.

Sexby There'll be no settlement based on terror and hatred.

Cromwell Sexby, you want the Stuarts back as much as the Irish do!

Sexby I don't seek a restoration. I am no royalist.

Cromwell Thurloe has evidence by the yard. You told Charles Stuart you could deliver him Portsmouth for £15,000. Deal and Ramsgate were cheaper. So I should think. Why, Sexby, why?

Sexby To ensure your death.

Cromwell And what solution will that bring?

Sexby At your death no-one will agree who should succeed you. The whole state will be in confusion. The people will rise, and all things will be brought to a true republic again.

Cromwell You're a simpleton, Sexby. The people will not rise. The people are sick of war. They want peace and strong government. They want — God save us all — for me to be king.

Sexby Where?

Cromwell What?

Sexby Where did the people meet to decide this?

Cromwell There needs no great assemblies bullied by sharp-tongued lawyers. The people are sick of change. They do not love the Stuarts.

Sexby They do not love you.

Cromwell They want to return to the old ways.

Sexby No, Cromwell, it's you who want to return to the old ways. You liked the idea of change—you were every radical's friend. But you're like every reformer who seizes power. You go to bed a republican and wake up a tyrant.

Cromwell You're wrong, Sexby. The god I worship is a god of change. But you would be forever overturning with no thought of how to fill the void. That is not reason, that is not justice.

Sexby My god is not a god of unreason, or madness, or tyranny. Consider what is justice and what is mercy and what is good, and I conclude that is of God.

Cromwell I love what you say with all my heart—but it has brought nothing but disaster. For every man that has a different notion of goodness and justice there is a different god.

Sexby We were all once agreed about what is just.

Cromwell But no longer. Oh, all men desire to have justice and liberty, but none will give it. Nothing will satisfy them unless they can put their fingers upon their brother's consciences and throttle them there. I tell you this nation seems agreed on one thing only — monarchy.

Sexby They fought to be rid of the last one.

Cromwell Charles's head was not taken off because he was a king, but because he did not perform his trust. If he had ruled justly, there would have been no civil war, no revolution, and I'd now be a farmer, and you'd be a ——?

Sexby Lawyer's clerk.

Cromwell And I would to God we were.

Sexby And so you must be king. Only eight years since we declared the First Year of Freedom. And we all know where we are when King Cromwell opens Parliament, and approves bills, and passes on his way to Windsor. We kneel before him and sleep the better because our property is safe. God save the King!

Cromwell Those who took up arms for Parliament in '42 would have approved this settlement.

Sexby But not those who declared a republic in '49. Thousands of us who fought to recover our birthright as Englishmen. Poor and mean soldiers gave their lives for a republic. I see now we ventured all for a cause that was never yours. You should have told us then, Cromwell. You would have had fewer under your command.

Lambert bursts into the room

Lambert I knew it! As soon as I found him gone, I knew where he'd be.

Cromwell And here I am, unharmed, unexploded.

Lambert He shall tell us his friends in England.

Cromwell No torture, Lambert.

Lambert glares

I shall visit him to make sure.

Lambert Guards! (*He pulls Sexby towards the door*)

Sexby You should have told us then, Cromwell.

Lambert bundles him out

Lambert You're not safe, Noll.

Cromwell Don't worry, John. I'm not to die at an assassin's hand. Nor in battle. But in my bed … (*He lies on the bed*) Or some bed. Naked and unmourned.

Lambert Are you unwell, Noll?

Cromwell No more than usual. The stone, pains in my bowels, giddiness. One of them will get me. Oh, I wish this storm were over! What do you want?

Lambert (*producing a paper*) This petition was given to me. Signed by over a hundred officers.

Cromwell Read it.

Lambert (*reading*) "We the undersigned have hazarded our lives against monarchy, and are still ready to do so, in defence of the liberties of this nation."

Cromwell Did you write this?

Lambert No.

Cromwell Who did?

Lambert I don't know.

Cromwell Thurloe will find out.

Lambert I would hazard — Colonel Pride.

Cromwell Why?

Lambert I've heard him boast that if you take the crown, he'll shoot you himself.

Cromwell Have you arrested him?

Lambert He was in his cups.

Cromwell Oh well, we may excuse a drunken assassin! Go on.

Lambert (*reading*) "We therefore humbly desire you to continue steadfast to the Old Cause, for the preservation of which we are most ready to lay down our lives …"

Cromwell (*savagely*) The Cause! The Cause! Everything has changed since we fought for the "Good Old Cause". Will the army never understand this?

Lambert The army understand that they fought to be rid of monarchy. If you take the crown I cannot swear to their loyalty.

Cromwell Have a care, Lambert. The army is my creature, not yours, and I know that they fought for a godly England.

Lambert Hardly!

Cromwell Maybe not at first, but God brought it to that issue in the end. Victory lies in obeying God.

Lambert But Noll, it's years since God has told you what to obey! And you know why? Because you're attempting the impossible.

Cromwell How?

Lambert You believe in property and the social order?

Cromwell nods

So do I. And you strive for a godly nation?

Cromwell With all my heart.

Lambert The two can never be brought together. How can you erect a godly England when you still have landlord and tenant? Does a man with five thousand pound a year truly consider himself an equal before Christ with a man with fifty?

Cromwell I do.

Lambert But you are one in a thousand. Trust me. I travel the country, and I know men's hearts. When the great Day of Judgement comes, the rich man may stand in terror, but till that hour he hoards his gold with pride. Christ may preach that we should hold all things in common, but it is the path to anarchy and ruin.

Cromwell The revolution was never about holding all in common.

Lambert Sexby and his like thought it was.

Cromwell The people never did.

Lambert But the people didn't make the revolution. The army did. The army defeated Charles, arrested him, executed him.

Cromwell (*his frustration breaking out*) But how can the army find a way of governing by the people's consent? That is the great question. Can an army set up a democracy?

Lambert In time. This army represents the people's interests more than this present Parliament ...

Cromwell But the people don't accept that. Consent is the cornerstone, and England will never consent to being ruled by an army.

Lambert But Noll, you've never governed by consent! You've no notion what the people want. Oh, you may have done thirty years ago when you farmed the Fens, but now you're sealed off in Whitehall, swaddled in ignorance. I tell you you're a government sitting on the sword and the musket — and that is why your parliamentary republic is failing.

Cromwell My republic may be … faltering, but the people long for settlement.

Lambert Then there is a way forward.

Cromwell What?

Lambert Nominate me as your successor — as Protector. And I would govern through a council.

Cromwell Chosen by?

Lambert Myself.

Cromwell And Parliament?

Lambert Would meet every three years and vote the taxes we needed.

Cromwell And if they refused?

Lambert Oh, Parliament can debate, squabble, air their grievances, but they will come to heel.

Cromwell You'd be a tyrant.

Lambert There is only one way to nurture a revolution, if the people do not yet understand it. And that is dictatorship. For a time at least.

Cromwell Then you and I will never agree.

Lambert Why not? You're a dictator now, if you would but own it. (*Desperately*) Noll, you must think of the people who come after you. Don't abandon us. Twenty years of army rule may be a small price, if the people come to accept the revolution. It'll be my life's work — I care for nothing else.

Cromwell (*obdurate*) I rule through Parliament, and whatever title they thrust upon me, I am still no tyrant. God will judge which of us is right.

A beat. Lambert realizes he may have gone too far

Lambert Let's not fall out, Noll. Too much depends on us. (*Beat*) You and I can quarrel — and no harm done. You used to call me the son you should have had.

Beat

Four years ago you stayed at Wimbledon, and told Frances she would one day be first lady in the land.

Cromwell looks at him sharply

And you would like that to be, I know. Come and see us?

Cromwell That's not possible. (*Beat*) Lambert, I shall need you to take an oath of loyalty.

Lambert To you?

Cromwell To me. Your petition has warned me. Whether I be Protector or king, I shall require all my officers to swear obedience.

Pause

Lambert Take the crown then. But it won't save us. King Richard won't last a year. Once one royal family has been deposed, the next may follow suit. Oh, you'll stay our Moses. But the people are waiting for Moses to die, and when he does "they shall corrupt all his work". Only the army can save England — and you're too much of an Englishman to let them. I resign all my offices and appointments from this moment.
Cromwell I am not asking you to do that.
Lambert I can see you've done with me.

Cromwell does not reply

I shall tend my garden.

Cromwell nods

May I give your love to Frances?

Cromwell nods

You should nominate your successor. The choice is simple now.

Lambert exits

Cromwell Dowland!

Hingston plays Dowland's "Melancholy Galliard". Cromwell seems close to collapse

No, no. That's the most melancholy thing he ever wrote. Play me something with spirit.

Hingston plays a Byrd "Battle" piece

Better. (*He signs a letter*) God knows what I'm signing. Thurloe could have granted himself Wales for all I know.

Bettie bursts in, followed by Marvell

Bettie Fanny doesn't like it.
Cromwell Like what?
Bettie "Cynthia and Endymion". Her wedding masque — with you as Jove.
Cromwell Why not?
Bettie She says she can't act, can't sing.
Cromwell She is my daughter.
Bettie And she hates the name Cynthia. Cynthia!
Cromwell I don't like Cynthia.
Bettie You would if you were called Bettie. Oh, do stop that terrible noise!

The music stops

That's better. Oh, I've insulted him. I'm sorry, Mr Hingston, you play
beautifully. The tune's just not worthy of you.

A trill of accord

Cromwell I liked it.
Bettie It's bad for your heart. The point is Fanny doesn't want any play. She
  wants ——
Cromwell Fifty violins.
Bettie Yes. And fifty trumpets. And she wants dancing ——
Cromwell Dancing!
Bettie Mixed dancing, men and women.
Cromwell Mixed ...
Bettie Till dawn. I said you'd never agree.
Cromwell And no masque?
Bettie No.
Cromwell So I wouldn't be Jove?
Bettie I'm afraid not.
Cromwell It's the first good news I've had today. She can have her dancing.
Bettie You mean ... Fanny can have her wedding?

Cromwell nods

To Robert?
Cromwell To Robert Rich.
Bettie Oh thank you. And it means Andrew can devote himself to the cruelty
  of the Spaniards.
Cromwell No he can't. No more dancing baboons. He'll be too busy
  assisting Milton.
Bettie He has the job?
Cromwell If he stops writing poetry.

Marvell Henceforth I write nothing but prose.
Cromwell And no plays.
Marvell No, Your Highness.
Cromwell You might get elected for Hull yet.

Thurloe hurries in

Thurloe Your Highness, Blake found the Spanish fleet. In the Canaries off
   Santa Cruz.
Cromwell And captured them?
Thurloe Destroyed them.
Cromwell The treasure?
Thurloe At the bottom of the ocean.

Beat

Cromwell And Blake?
Thurloe Admiral Blake died within sight of Plymouth.

Beat

Cromwell He's found his release.
Marvell I wish all the treasures of the Indies were in an ocean grave.
Cromwell Why?
Marvell So should war's chief support be buried with them. And the land
   owe her peace unto the sea.
Thurloe It's a disaster. We need the gold.
Cromwell No, Marvell speaks the truth. That's why I've given him the job.
Thurloe Without consulting me?
Cromwell Ay. And Lambert's resigned. Also without consulting you.
Thurloe I know. It saves us seven thousand a year. I've stopped his
   payments.
Cromwell He's barely left the building.
Thurloe It's a lot of money, Your Highness. Nearly twenty pounds a day.
Cromwell Give him two thousand a year.
Thurloe He's resigned. We can't afford ——
Cromwell Out of my own money.
Thurloe If Your Highness insists.

A highly indignant Frances bursts in

Frances You've dismissed him! (*She becomes aware of how full the room
   is, but ploughs on*) There was no need for that.

Cromwell He resigned.
Frances You forced him.
Thurloe I don't think, Lady Lambert, this is the time to ——
Frances It is very much the time. The Protector promised me time today.
Bettie Father is tired and unwell ——
Cromwell Leave us.
Bettie But, Father ——
Cromwell It's true. I promised her. Leave us.

Bettie pointedly kisses Cromwell and then leaves, followed by Thurloe and Marvell

Frances John takes back his resignation.
Cromwell Is that his wish?
Frances It will be. Why have you quarrelled?
Cromwell That you must ask John.
Frances Coward.

But Cromwell does not react

Do you know what I admired most in you?
Cromwell What?
Frances Your frenzy.
Cromwell Not easy to live with.
Frances Easy for me. You wrestled for the truth. You were drunk with it.
And when you saw the way clear, you drove everyone, everything before
you.
Cromwell The way clear — has deserted me of late.
Frances Oh Noll, what does it matter whether you're Protector or king?
What are titles to you?
Cromwell Feathers in a bonnet.

They both laugh

Frances It's power that matters — and that you have tenfold. Power is
enough to nominate your successor.
Cromwell Parliament wants a royal family.
Frances What do you care for parliament? (*Imitating him*) "Dolts and
imbeciles."
Cromwell The people want it.
Frances "Fools and silly gazers."
Cromwell Frances, the only way to keep the Stuarts out is for me to take the
crown.

Frances I don't believe it. You can do whatever you please. The Lord has
smiled on you.

Cromwell Not any longer.

Frances You're the greatest leader this country has ever known.

Cromwell God is punishing me.

Frances Why do you say that?

Cromwell He has raised me so high. Why? To tempt me? To test me? And
now he has left me. Why? To punish me. What for? The sins of my youth? ·

Frances Noll, I can't believe your youth was very wicked.

Cromwell Oh, I was a chief — the chief of sinners. I loved darkness and I
hated light. This is true. Drunkenness, covetousness, fornication ... I hated
godliness, yet God had mercy on me. He brought me low for many months.
I couldn't rise from my bed. I was only twenty-eight, and I thought I was
going mad. And then — he lifted that terrible melancholy from me. He
raised me from the shadow of death. Why?

Frances He had a purpose for you.

Cromwell But what?

Frances He chose you to be our Moses — to lead us to the promised land.

Cromwell God prevented Moses from entering the promised land because
he'd disobeyed him. He died in the wilderness.

Frances But he set his people on their way. As you have done.

Cromwell No, they corrupted all his work. And I thought once that God had
a purpose for England ...

Frances That its people should be a pattern to all the world.

Cromwell Frances, the people of England — are a pattern of greed and self-
seeking. Oh, they may attend church, but only in body, not in mind. I called
for a rebirth, a reformation. I called for national days of prayer and fasting.
It's like shouting into the wind.

Frances They need time. The godly will show them.

Cromwell The godly! Who are the godly?

Frances Those who would build Jerusalem here in England.

Cromwell And would they even agree where to place the walls? Their
godliness has degenerated into the malice of the self-righteous. Their
jealousies and lies turn all to wormwood.

Frances What jealousies?

Cromwell They dispute doctrine as keenly as any Jesuit, and then persecute
any who disagree — even by a scruple. There are Christians who would
brand, maim, even tear out the tongues of fellow worshippers.

Frances But none of this is your doing. You have brought only healing and
understanding.

Cromwell But I shared their dream, their arrogance. I had this belief that I
was marked out, that I was the Godly Prince, sitting upon the throne,
proclaiming Christ's kingdom on earth, with Parliament and the army on
my right and left hand.

Frances That was a dream. God doesn't punish us for our dreams.

Cromwell But I *believed* God had so favoured me that there was nothing I could not do. I was drunk, ay drunk with the Holy Spirit. If King Charles saw himself as David, then I saw myself as Moses. Where's the difference?

Frances All the difference in the world. Charles forced narrow doctrine on us. You speak of a broad national church.

Cromwell God punished the king, and now he's punishing me. He has taken away his voice, his favour, his providence, which was once so clear. He has laughed at my little mightiness, and he has humbled me ...

Frances When the king died England was torn in spirit. Nothing in men's hearts but "overturn, overturn, overturn". We were in the wilderness, and you were the man ...

Cromwell No more of Moses, I beg you! It is not for us to assert how long we shall remain in the wilderness, or who shall take us forward. Perhaps there is no promised land. Perhaps Christ will never come down among us again. My only certainty is that I have failed.

Frances How can you have failed? No man has ever wielded greater power in England. No general was ever more feared abroad.

Cromwell Power — fear ... What are these to Christ? Frances, where is the godly nation? Where is the true republic? As my power is great, so is my failure ...

Cromwell collapses on the floor

Frances Noll. Noll! (*She tries to revive him, but to no purpose*) Help us! Thurloe! Someone!

Thurloe runs into the room

Thurloe Let me see him.

Bettie, Richard and Marvell enter. They cluster round

Bettie Father!

Thurloe Loosen him at the throat. He must have air.

Bettie Don't leave us. Don't leave us.

Cromwell opens his eyes and stirs

Oh, praise be!

Cromwell (*staggering to his knees*) God, turn your face to me. I saw it so plain at Dunbar. All things point to my taking the crown ... I see that. The name of king is so great, so understood, so reverenced by the people. But why? Both king and commoner are poor creeping ants before your throne. Lord, I must tell you — I have learned something today: that good men do not swallow this title of king. And therefore I cannot believe it has your blessing. Whichever way I turned today — the title has stuck with me. And does yet stick. At best I should accept it doubtingly — and Christ teaches us what is so done is not of faith. I cannot restore that which providence has destroyed. I cannot. I cannot.

Cromwell walks out of the room

The others gaze at one another, taking in the fateful implications of this decision

The Lights fade

CURTAIN

WHAT HAPPENED NEXT

Cromwell remained Protector, but was re-installed like a monarch. Bettie had a boy, named Oliver, who lived less than a year. She died of cancer in August 1658, and Cromwell, heart-broken and already ill, died a month later on September 3rd. Fanny married Robert Rich, with violins, trumpets and mixed dancing, but he soon died after of consumption. She remarried, had a large family and lived till 1721. Marvell's *Cynthia and Endymion* was performed at the youngest daughter Mary's wedding in November 1657, probably with Cromwell as Jove.

Sexby died in the Tower of gaol fever in January 1658. Lambert did re-enter the army and politics in 1659, opposing General Monck and Charles Stuart, but the army would not turn to him. He was imprisoned in 1660, first on Guernsey and then at Plymouth, until his death in 1684, despite all Frances' efforts to get him released. She died in 1676. At Cromwell's death, it was claimed that he had verbally named Richard as his successor. Richard was accepted as Protector, but resigned within nine months, without a drop of blood split. After 1660 he spent twenty years in exile in France, painted a good deal, then returned to England, still in debt, and lived peacefully as Mr Clarke (though his identity was widely known) until his death in 1712.

In 1660 Cromwell's body was dug up and hanged at Tyburn (as were other regicides, living and dead). His skull, which was displayed for many years outside Westminster Hall, may now be in Sydney Sussex College, Cambridge, his old college. Thurloe and the rest of the Cromwell family survived the Restoration intact. Thurloe was arrested, but soon released on condition he helped the government on foreign policy. Marvell became M.P. for Hull for eighteen years, never married, and wrote mostly in prose. He died in 1678, and his poems were finally published in 1681 from papers found in his room by his housekeeper. They were largely neglected for the next two centuries.

Hingston, like most musicians, was given a court post by Charles II. *The Cruelty of the Spaniards in Peru* and *Francis Drake* were performed in 1658-9, with libretti by Davenant. It's not known if Cromwell attended. In 1660 Charles granted Davenant one of the two royal patents to run a theatre, but he did not continue his experiments with opera. Women were allowed on the stage. Mrs Coleman was not the last female opera singer.

FURNITURE AND PROPERTY LIST

ACT I

On stage: Bed. *On it*: bed covers in disarray. *Beside it*: **Cromwell**'s clothes
Table. *On it*: quill pen and ink
Chairs

Off stage: Papers, including two pamphlets and four handwritten sheets (**Thurloe**)
Tray with plate of turbot, dish of vegetables, bread, jug of ale, two
glasses (**Thurloe**)
Bag containing a golden orb and sceptre and great seal (**Thurloe**)

ACT II

Strike: Tray of food and drink, orb, sceptre, great seal and bag, four handwritten sheets (the Horation Ode)

Off stage: Papers (**Marvell**)
Papers (**Thurloe**)
Sword (**Cromwell**)

Personal: **Sexby**: hands bound with rope
Lambert: paper

LIGHTING PLOT

Property fittings required: nil

Interior. The same scene throughout

ACT I

To open: General interior lighting, dawn till noon

Cue 1	**Cromwell** ponders	(Page 30)
	Fade to black-out	

ACT II

To open: General interior lighting, 2p.m. till dusk

Cue 2	The others gaze at one another	(Page 57)
	Fade to black-out	

EFFECTS PLOT

ACT I

Cue 1	To open	(Page 1)
	Thunder; pause then loud clap of thunder; continue	
	storm sounds intermittently throughout Act	
Cue 2	**Cromwell** kneels by the bed. Pause	(Page 1)
	Key turns in the lock	

ACT II

Cue 3	To open Act	(Page 32)
	Thunder, continue storm sounds intermittently throughout	
	Act	

MUSIC PLOT

As the musician John Hingston is never seen, the harpsichord music could be live off stage, or recorded.

ACT I

Cue 1	**Cromwell**: "Hingston, are you there yet?" *Trill*	(Page 10)
Cue 2	**Cromwell**: "Play me something familiar" *"Gather ye Rosebuds" (Herrick)*	(Page 11)
Cue 3	**Cromwell**: "… William Lawes?" *Affirmative trill*	(Page 11)
Cue 4	**Cromwell**: "No Scheidt before breakfast." *"All in a Garden Green" (version of the "Diggers' Anthem") starts to play*	(Page 11)
Cue 5	**Cromwell**: "That's enough! I must work." *Cut "All in a Garden Green"*	(Page 11)
Cue 6	**Cromwell** sits at the table *"Scots March" banged out*	(Page 11)
Cue 7	**Cromwell**: "You choose. English." *Byrd fantasia*	(Page 22)

MADE AND PRINTED IN GREAT BRITAIN BY
LATIMER TREND & COMPANY LTD PLYMOUTH
MADE IN ENGLAND